einaudi glass tavener nyman yared

# the quiet room

barber hawes armstrong talbot

**Chester Music**
part of The Music Sales Group
London / New York / Paris / Sydney / Copenhagen / Berlin / Madrid / Tokyo

Published by
Chester Music Limited
14-15 Berners Street, London, W1T 3LJ, UK.

Exclusive Distributors:
Music Sales Limited
Distribution Centre, Newmarket Road,
Bury St Edmunds, Suffolk, IP33 3YB, UK.

Music Sales Pty Limited
120 Rothschild Avenue, Rosebery,
NSW 2018, Australia.

Order No. CH71489
ISBN 1-84609-631-6
This book © Copyright 2006 Chester Music Limited.

Edited by Ann Farmer.

Printed in the EU.

www.musicsales.com

Your guarantee of quality:
As publishers, we strive to produce every book
to the highest commercial standards.

The book has been carefully designed to
minimise awkward page turns and to make
playing from it a real pleasure.

Particular care has been given to specifying
acid-free, neutral-sized paper made from pulps
which have not been elemental chlorine bleached.

This pulp is from farmed sustainable forests
and was produced with special regard for
the environment.

Throughout, the printing and binding have
been planned to ensure a sturdy, attractive
publication which should give years of enjoyment.

If your copy fails to meet our high standards,
please inform us and we will gladly replace it.

# Alexandra Park

Composed by John Metcalfe

6

# Adagio For Strings

### (Featured in the film *Platoon*)

Composed by Samuel Barber

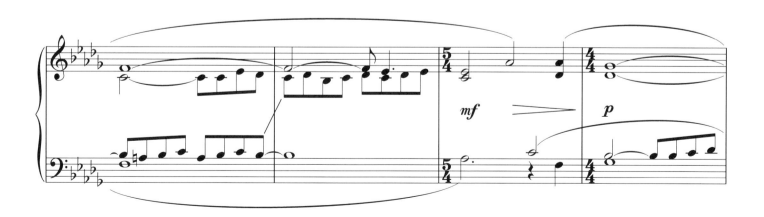

*(with increasing intensity)*

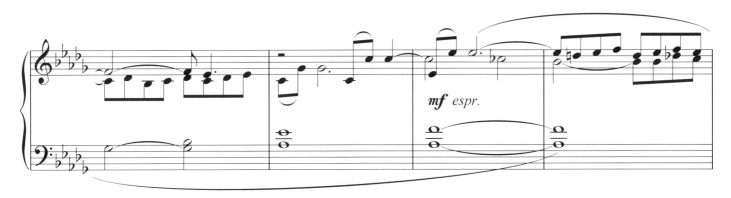

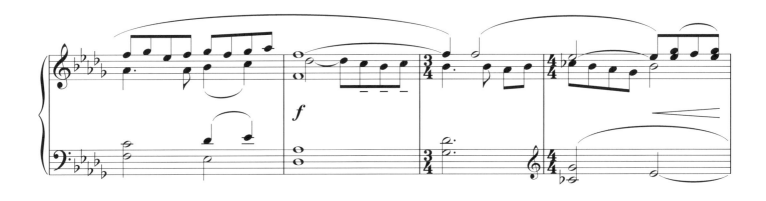

14

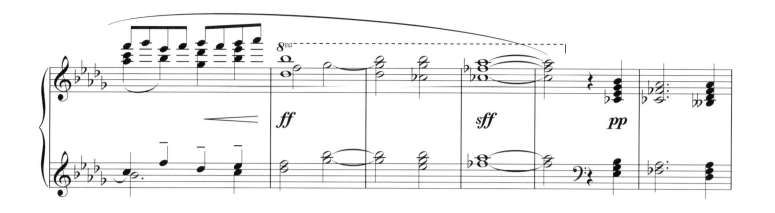

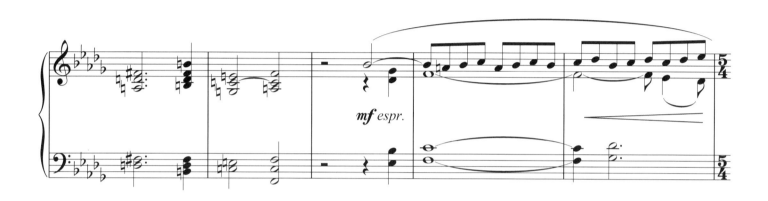

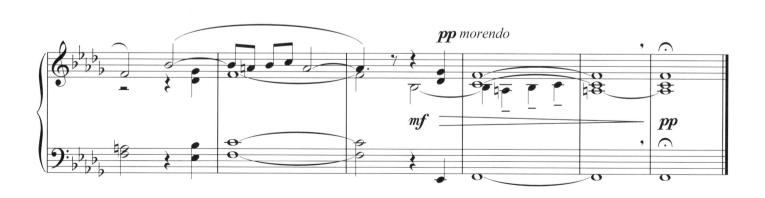

15

# Cumulonimbus

Composed by Joby Talbot

**Tempo I**

21

poco rall. - - - - - - - poco più mosso

22

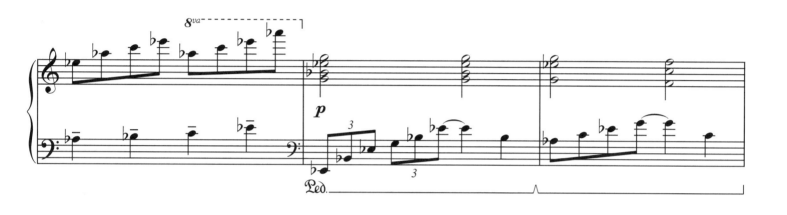

# Dolce Droga

Composed by Ludovico Einaudi

26

# Elegy

Composed by Chris Craker

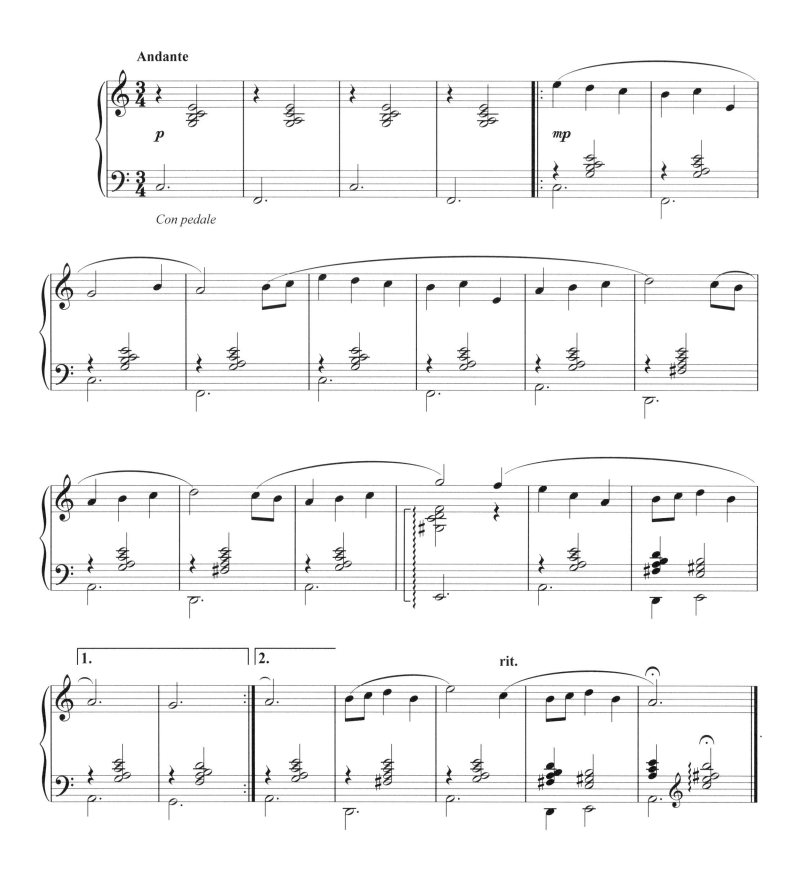

# Frozen

(From the film *Cashback*)

Composed by Guy Farley

# Eustace and Hilda

## (From the BBC dramatisation of L P Hartley's trilogy)

Composed by Richard Rodney Bennett

# Farewell

Composed by Zbigniew Preisner

**Andante sostenuto** ♩ = *c.* 72

*Con pedale*

poco a poco cresc.

rit.

mf

# Glassworks – opening

Composed by Philip Glass

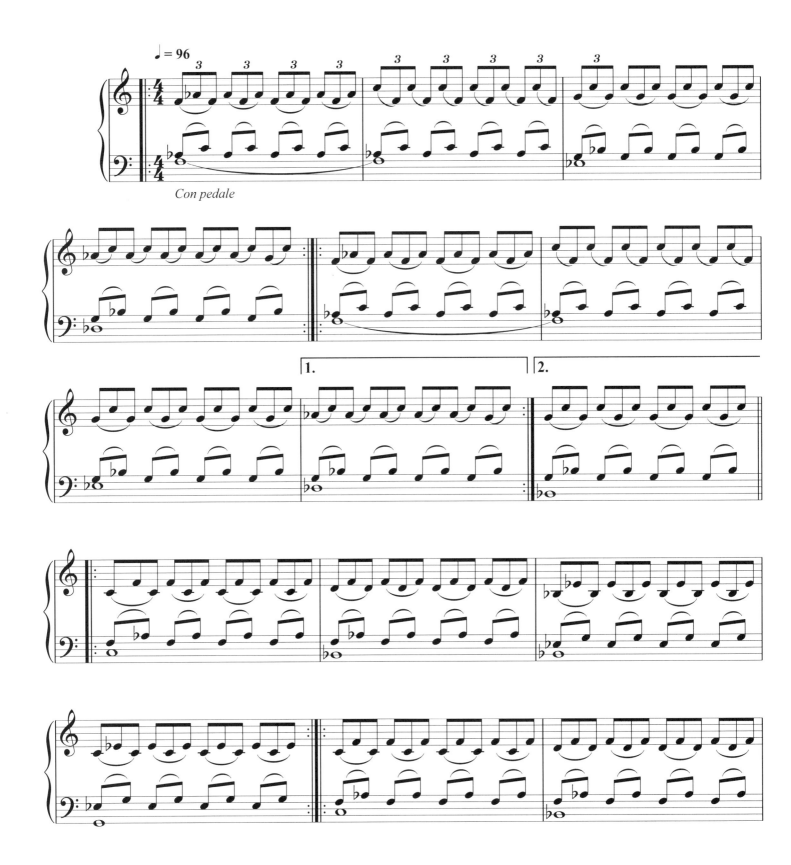

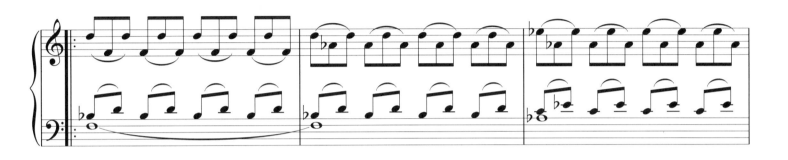

# Goodbye

Composed by Geoffrey Burgon

a tempo (but freely)

rall.

rit.

43

# The Heart Asks Pleasure First

(From the film *The Piano*)

Composed by Michael Nyman

♩. = 46 (con rubato)

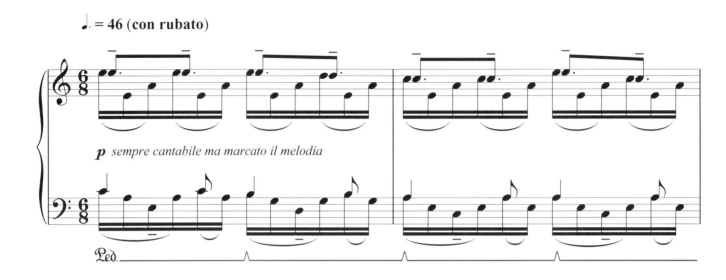

*p sempre cantabile ma marcato il melodia*

Ped.

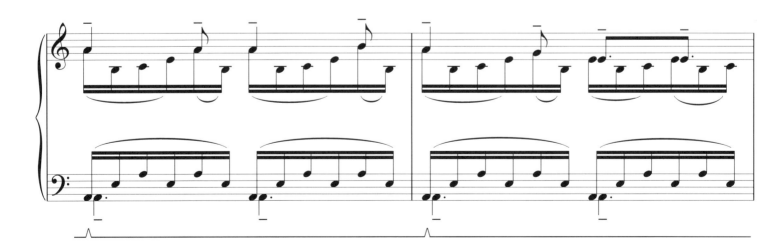

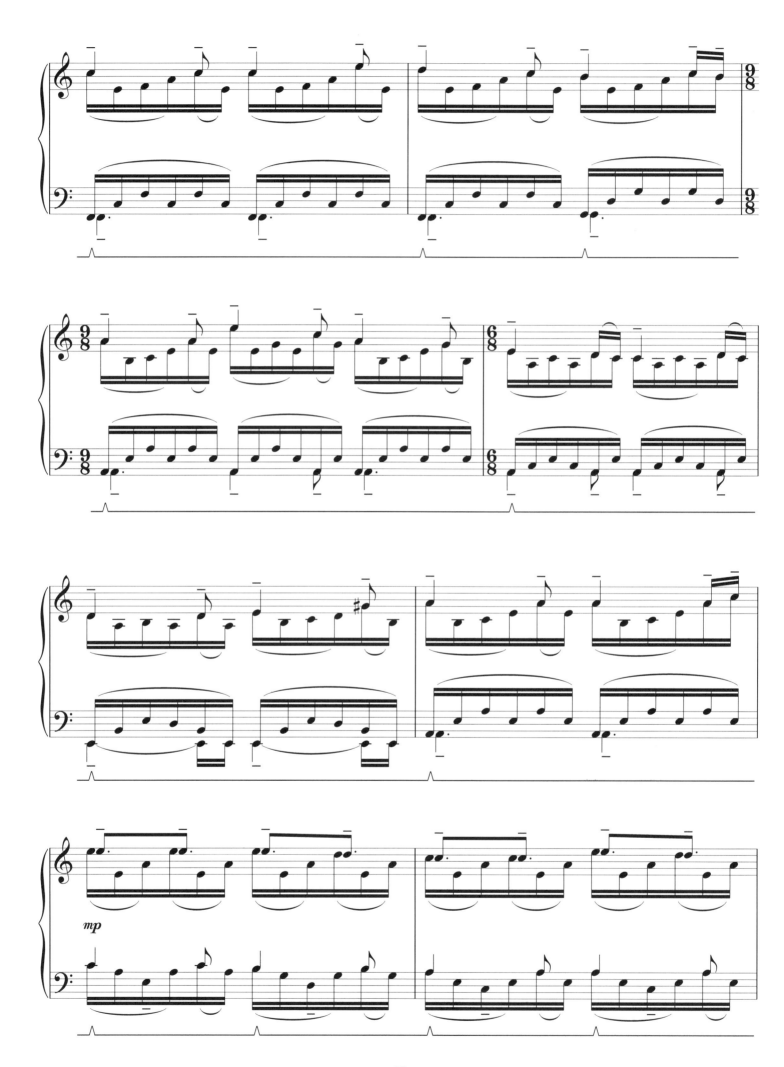

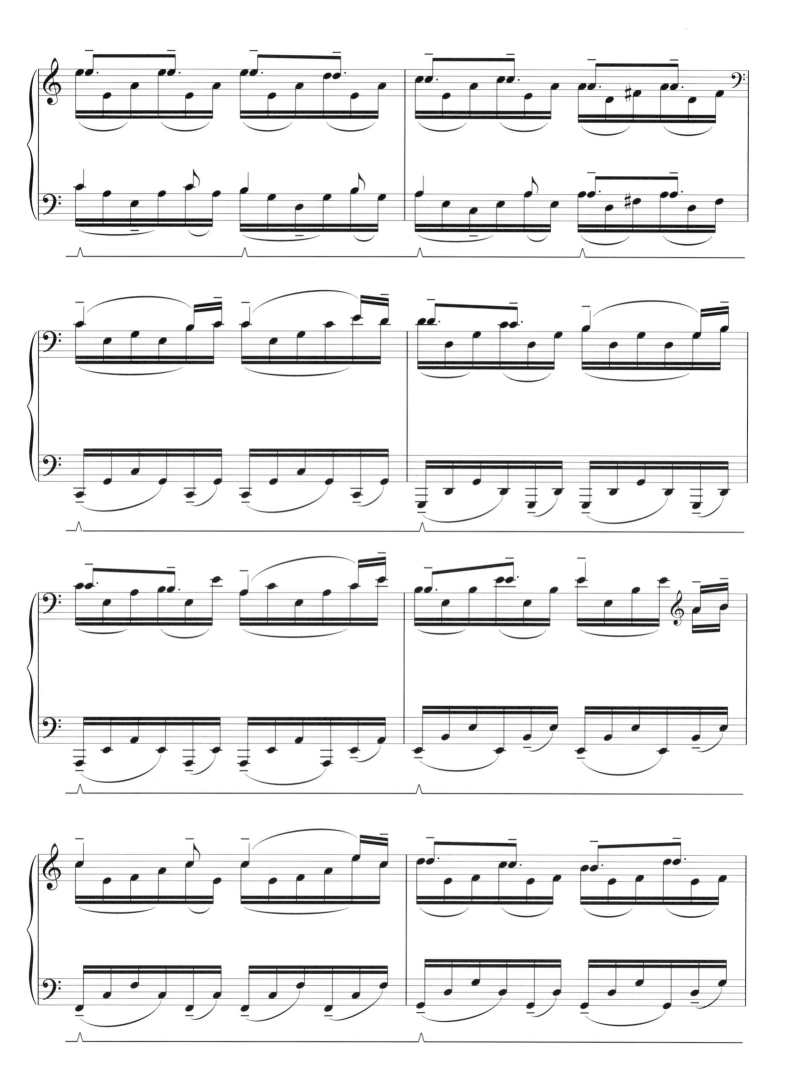

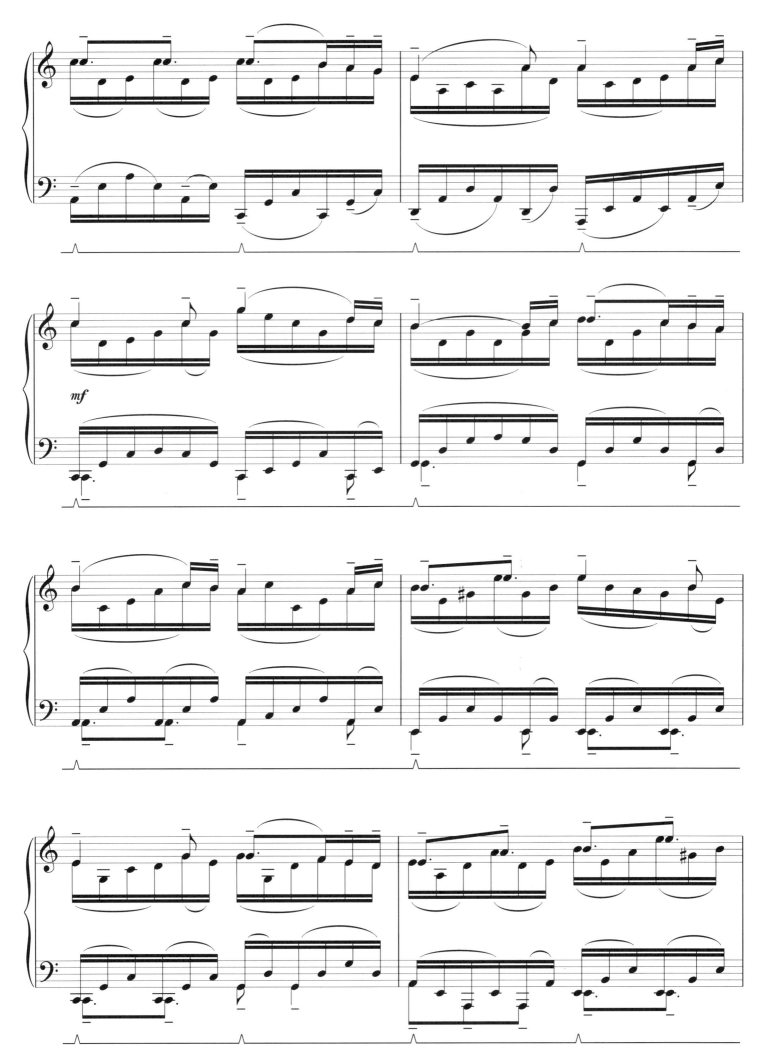

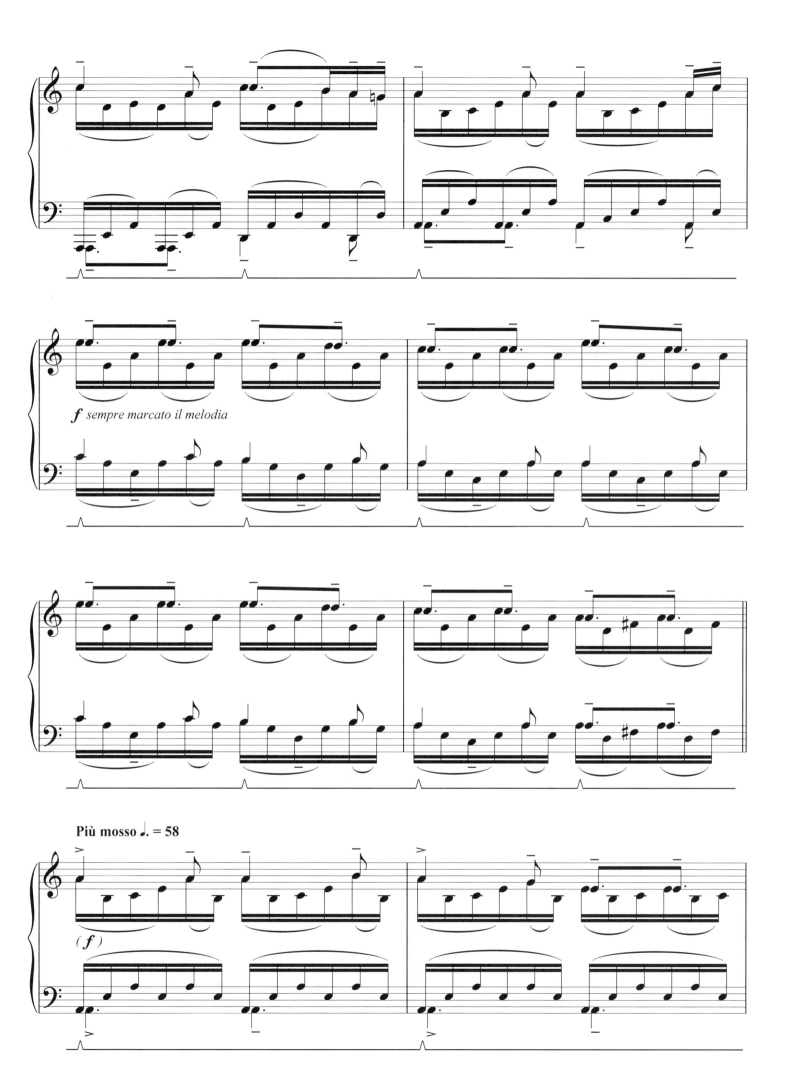

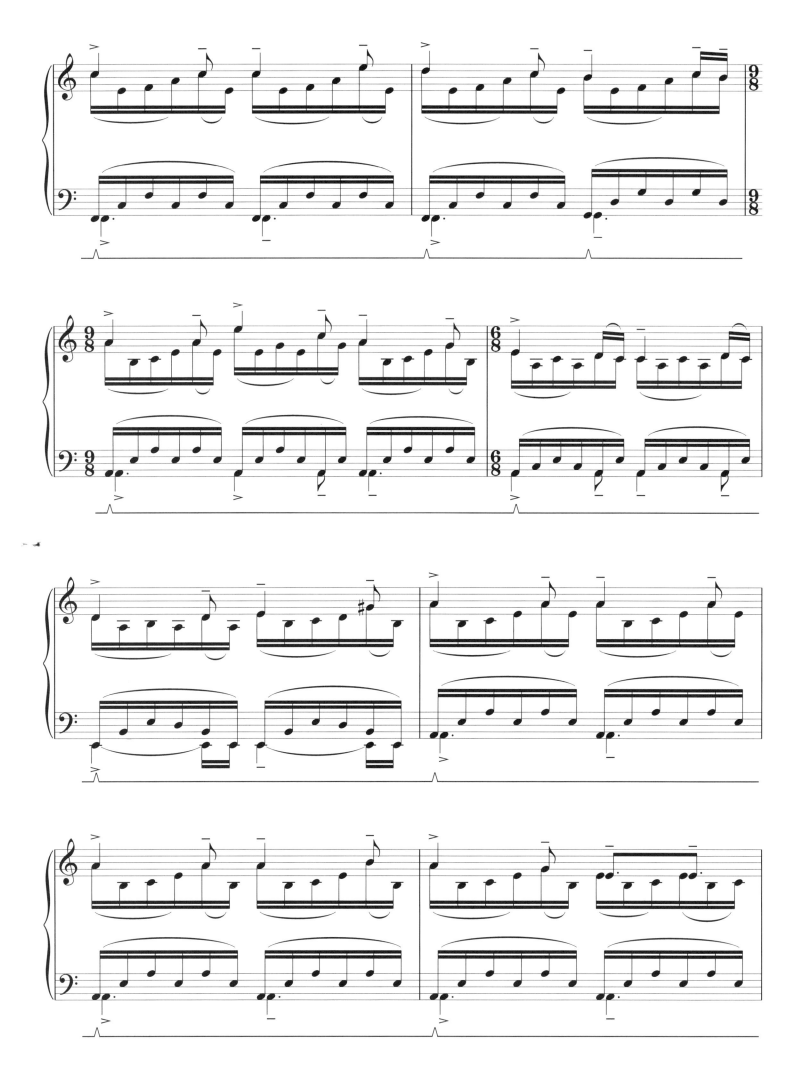

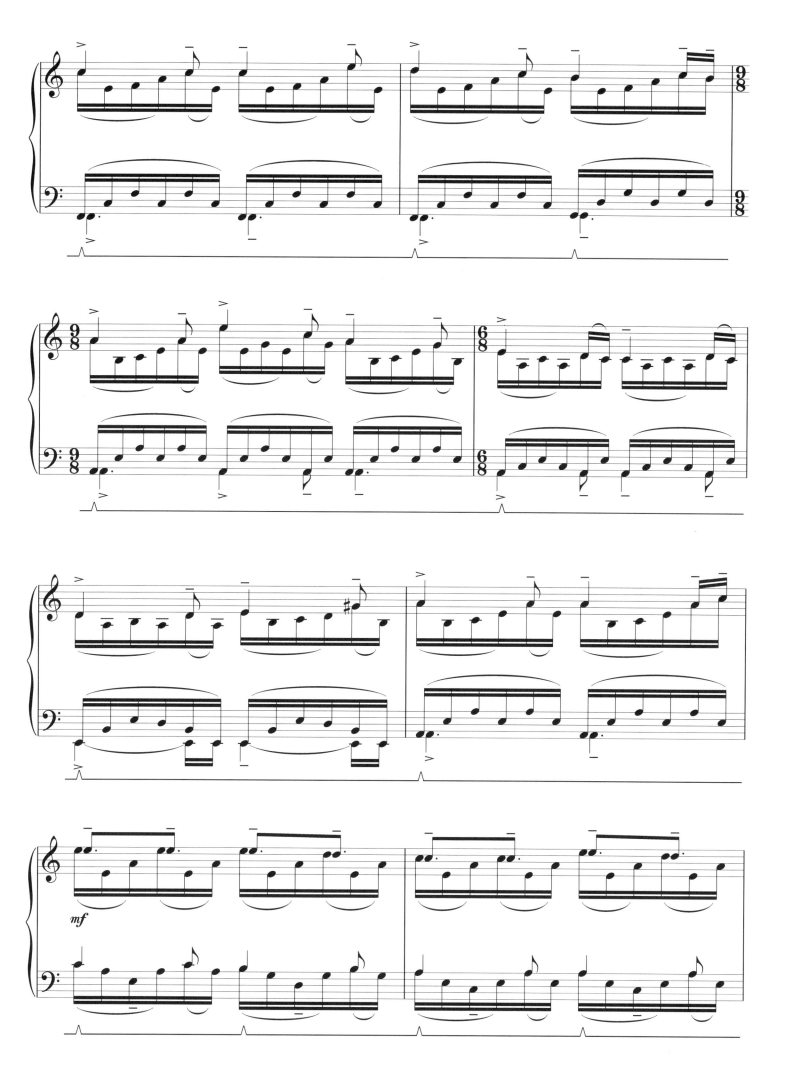

51

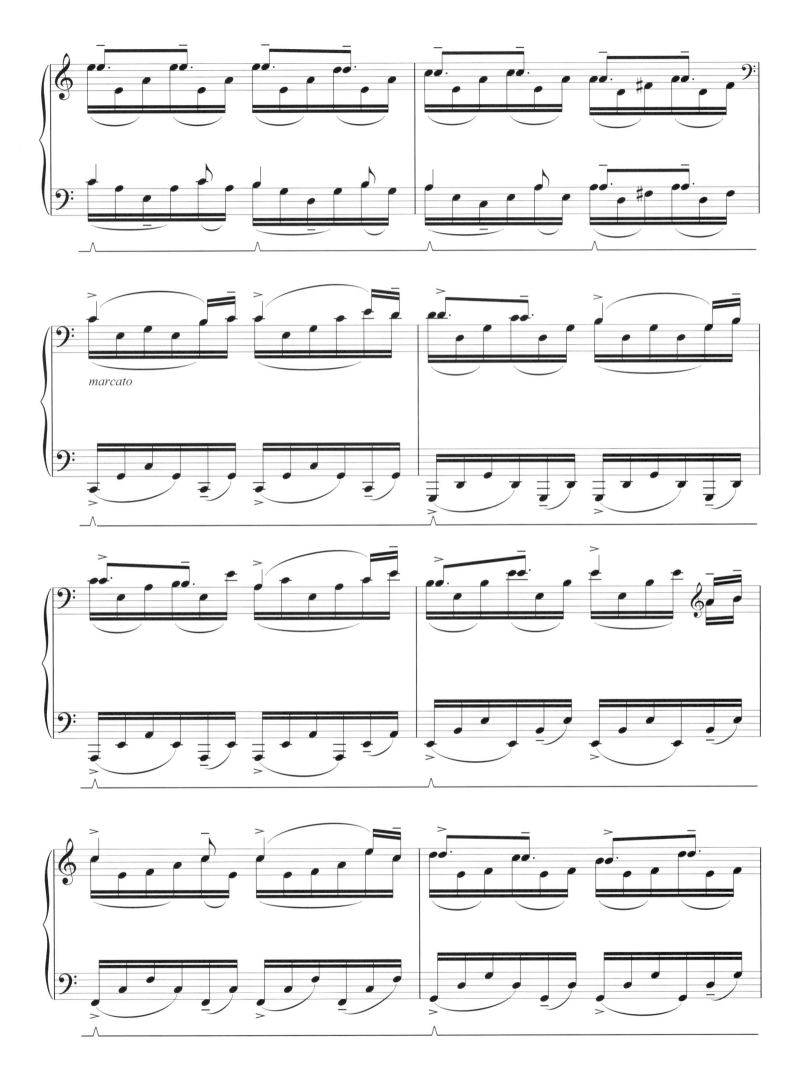

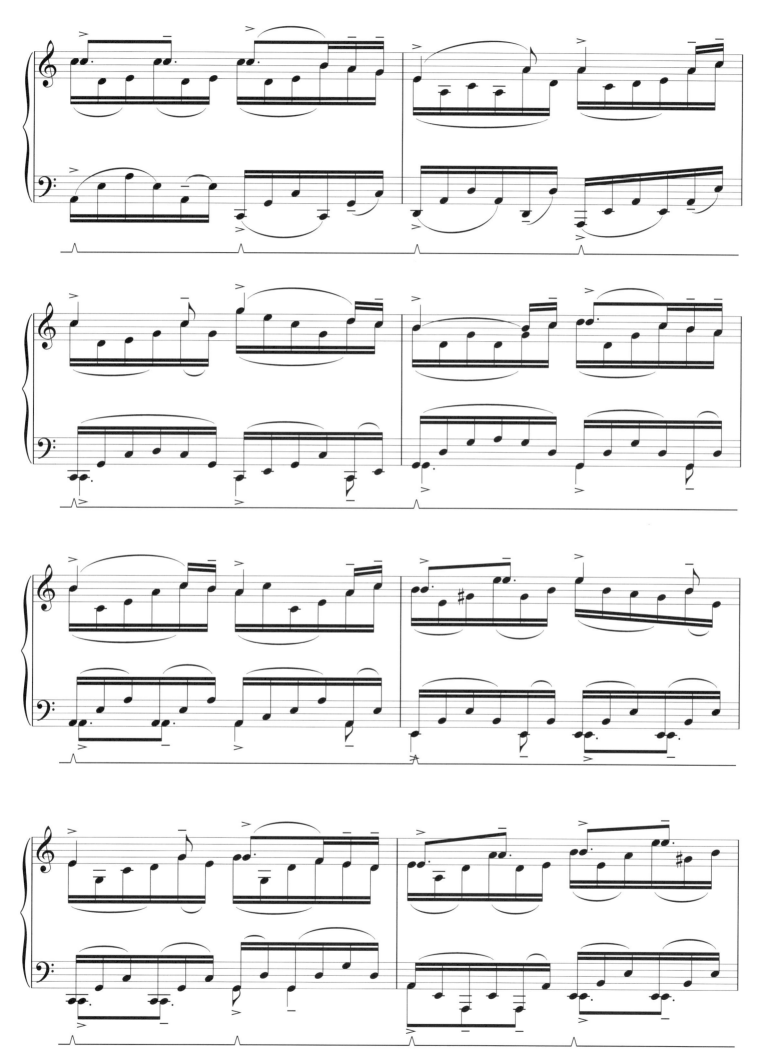

53

**Tempo I** ($\dot{\quad}$. = 46)

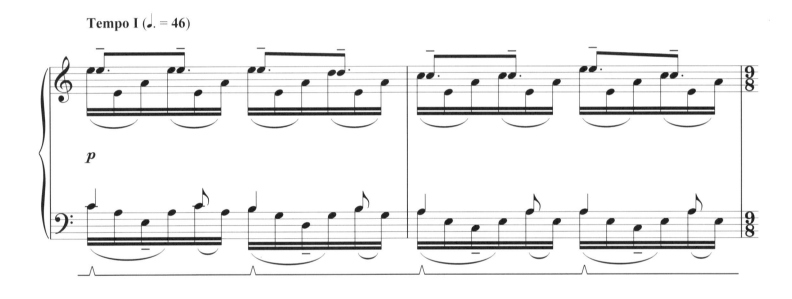

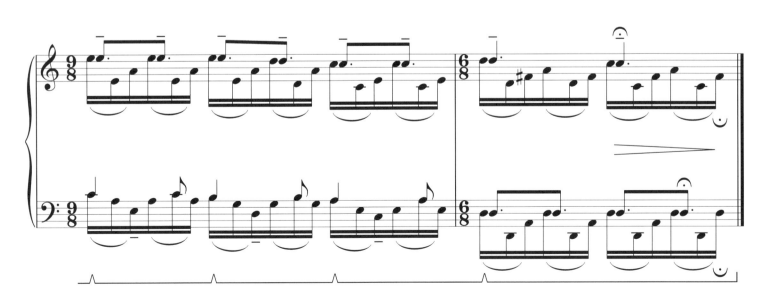

# Hush

Composed by Craig Armstrong

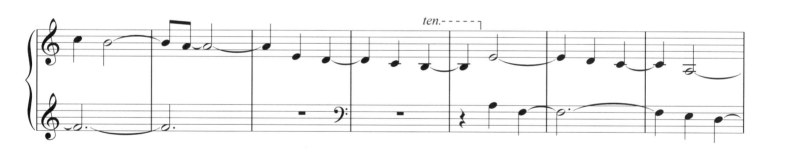

*poco dim.*

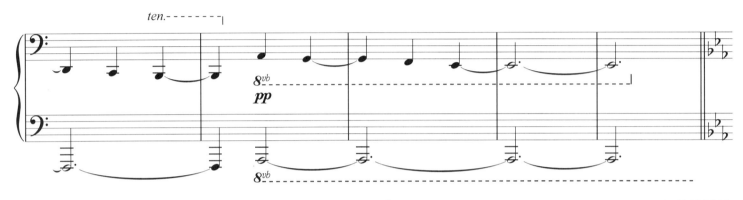

*ten.*

*pp*

**Tempo I**

*ff*

*pp*

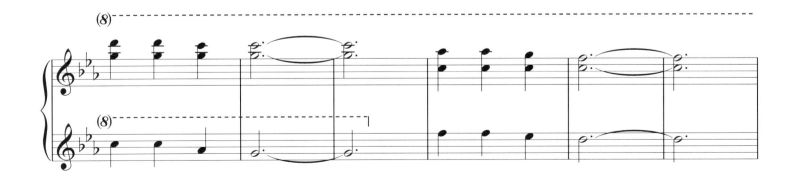

57

# If

(From the animated film *The Diary Of Anne Frank*)

Composed by Michael Nyman

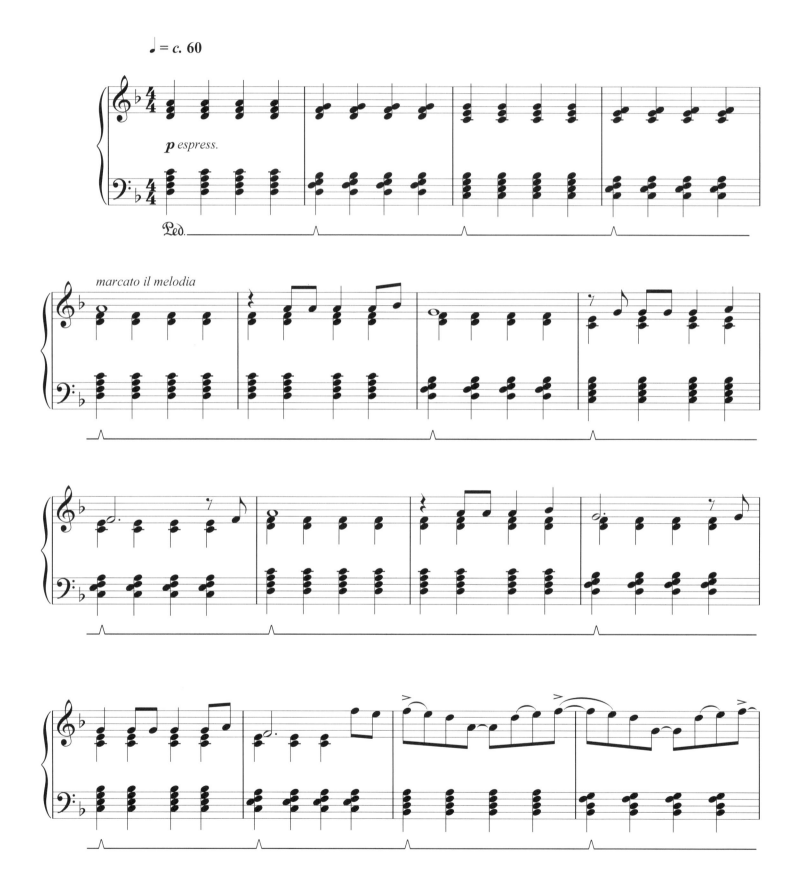

61

# Lines Of Desire

Composed by Tarik O'Regan

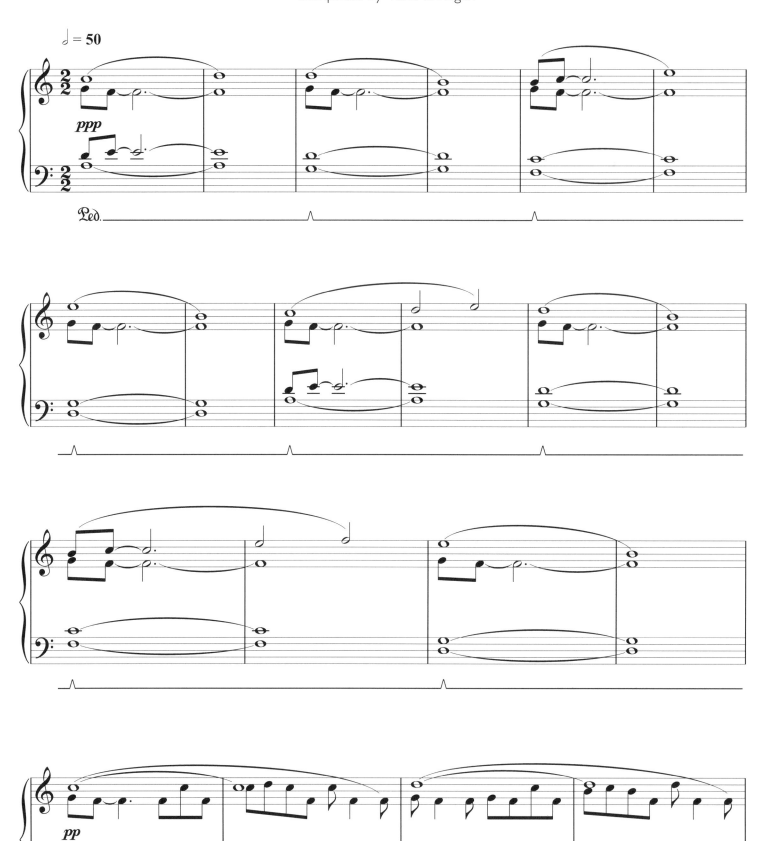

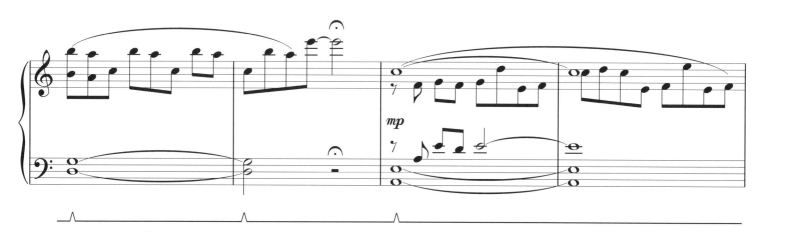

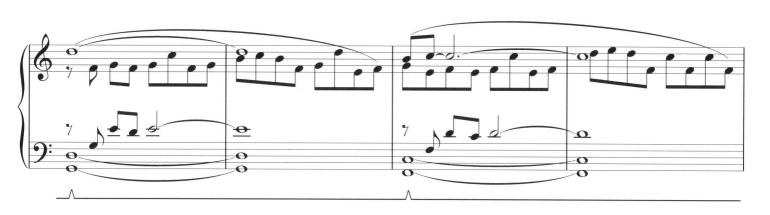

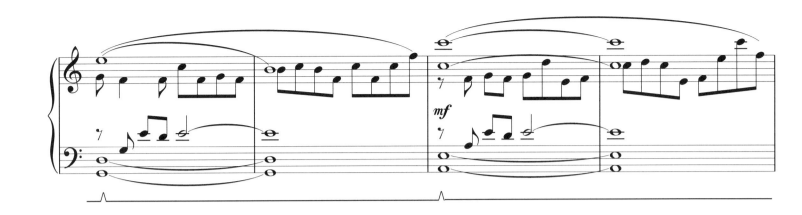

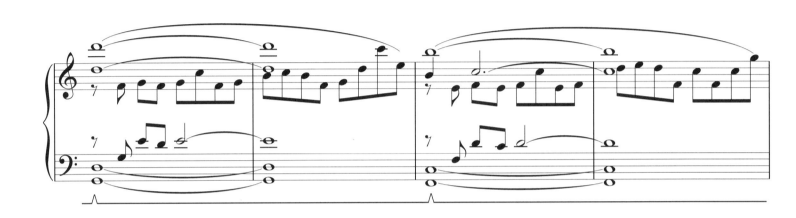

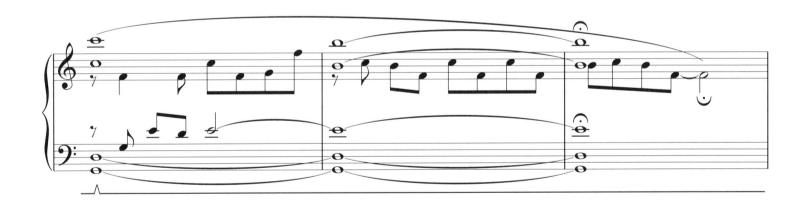

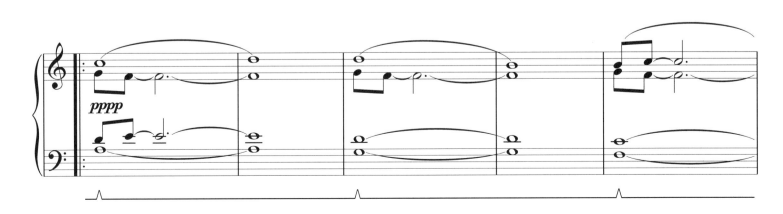

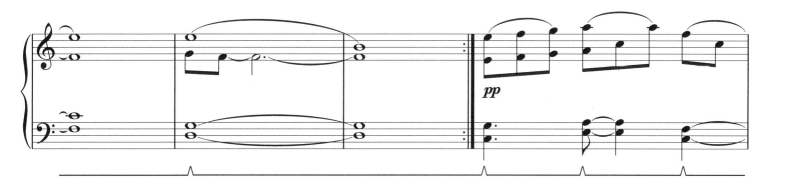

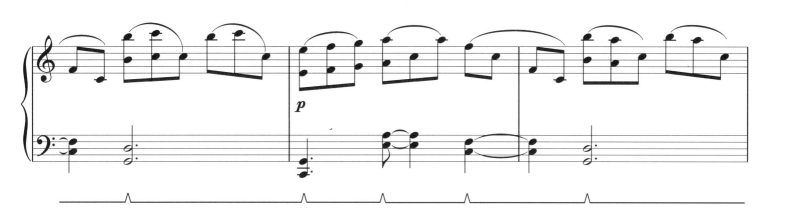

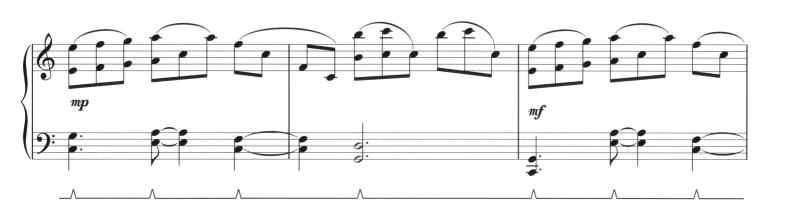

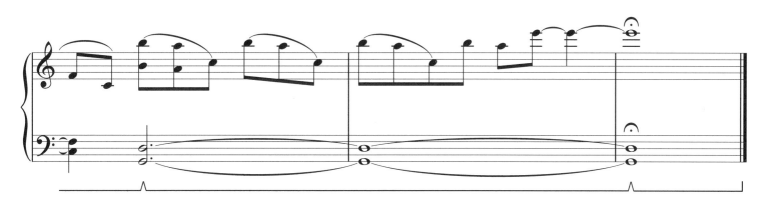

# The Lord's Prayer (1999)

Composed by Sir John Tavener

**Very still and serene** (♩ = c. 42)

*molto legato e cantabile*

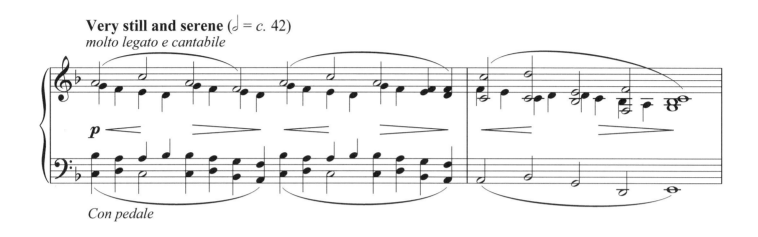

*Con pedale*

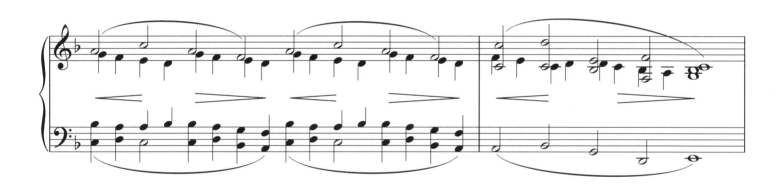

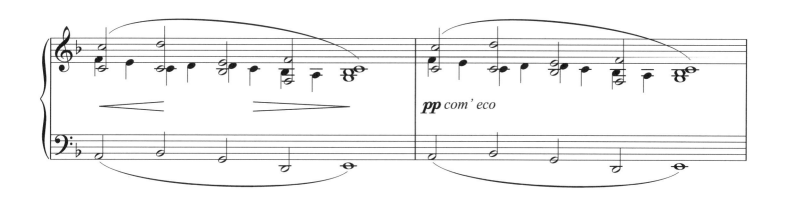

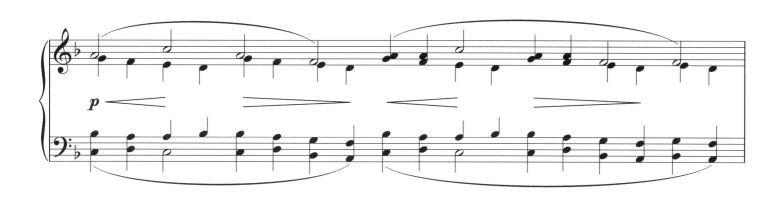

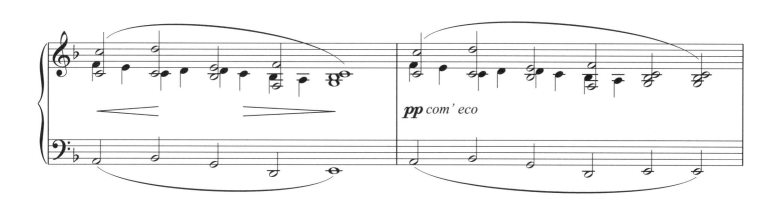

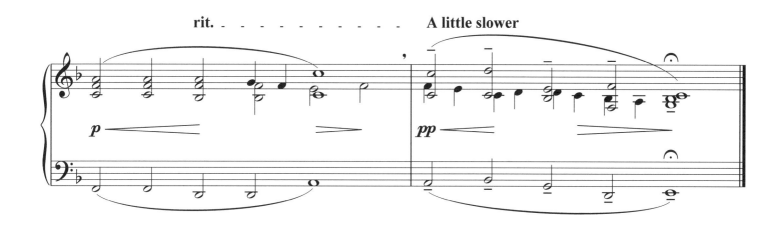

# Moving Ground

Composed by James Whitbourn

♩ = *c.* **60 (slow and gentle)**

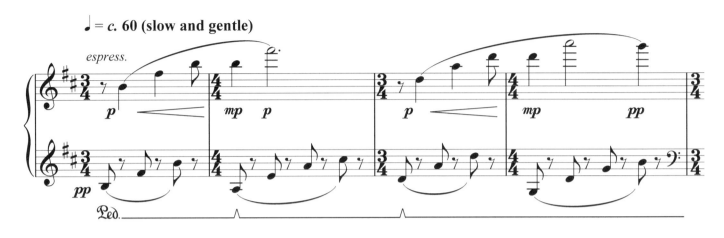

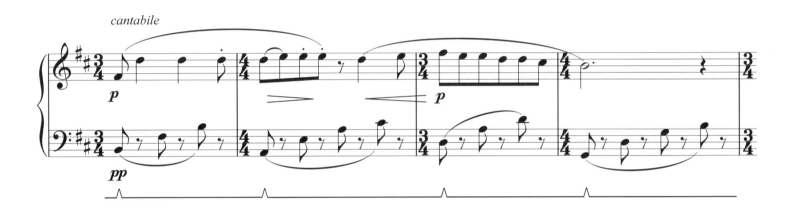

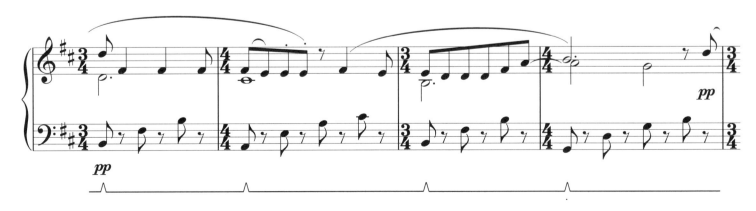

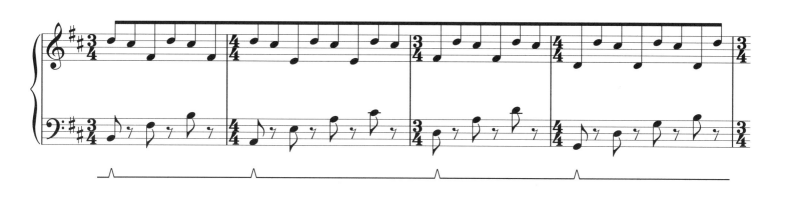

# Quanta Qualia

Composed by Patrick Hawes

# Questa Volta

Composed by Ludovico Einaudi

# The Quiet Room

Composed by Debbie Wiseman

Con pedale

# The Sentence

(From the film *Death On The Staircase*)

Composed by Jocelyn Pook

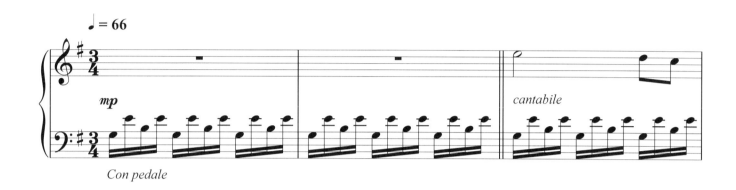

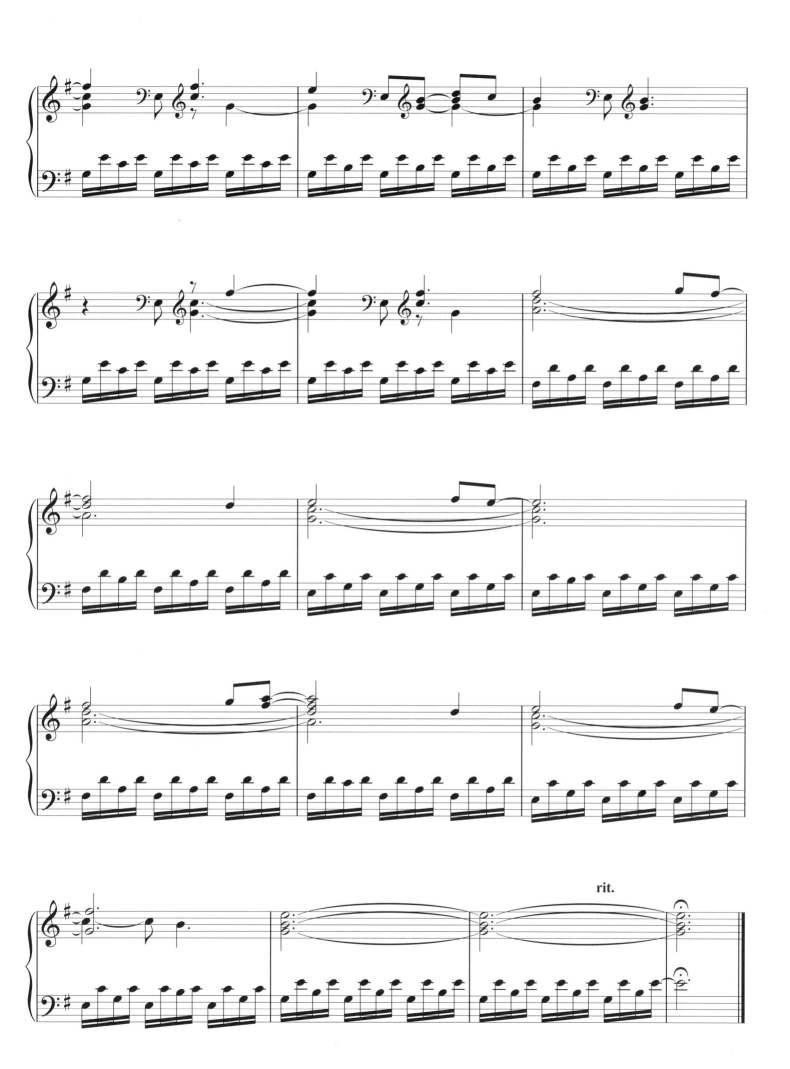

# Slow Mo

Composed by Chris Butler

# Song for a Raggy Boy

(From the film *Song for a Raggy Boy*)

Composed by Richard Blackford

rit.    a tempo

# Song for Rani

Composed by Gabriel Yared

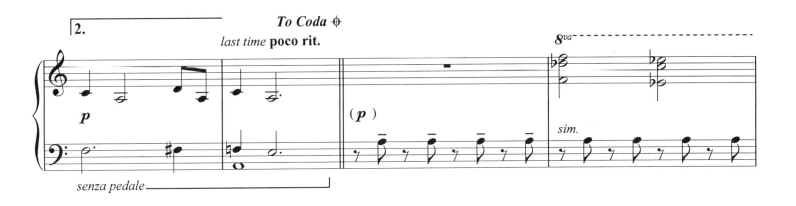

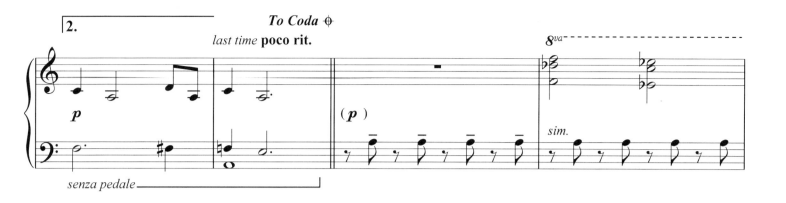

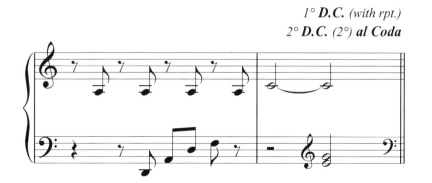

# Silencium

## (From the TV series *Silent Witness*)

Composed by John Harle

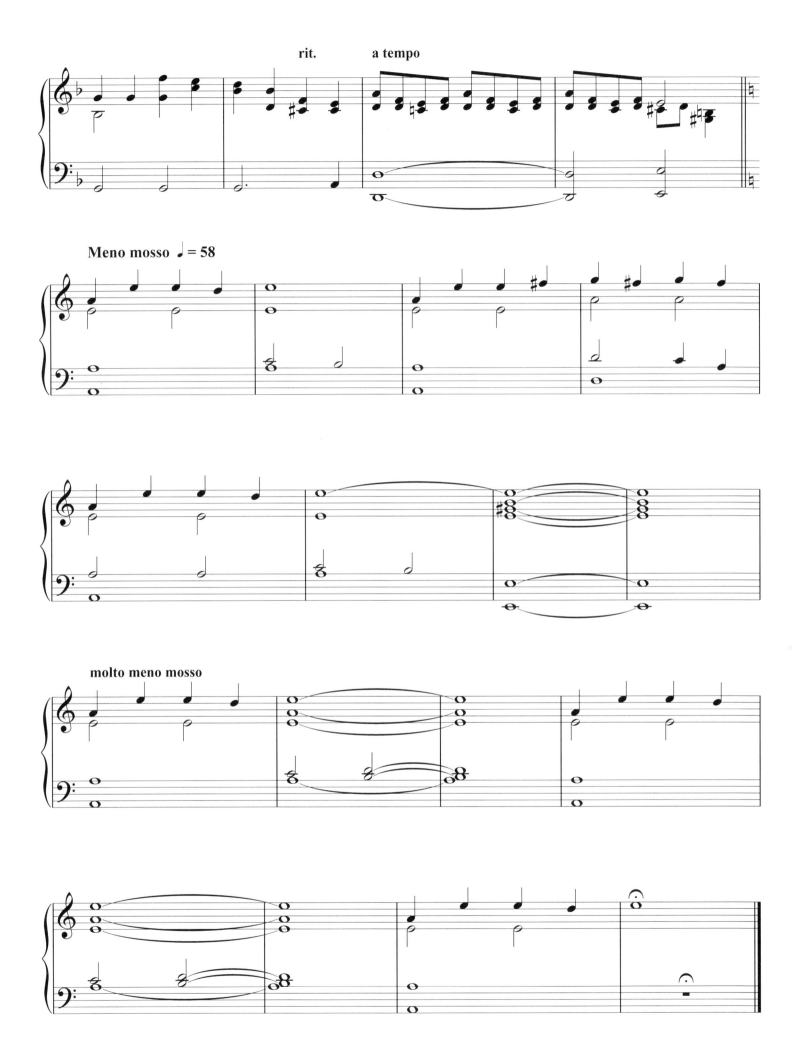